Growing Up Through Changes and Challenges

The Little Drop of Water

and

Leafy the Leaf

Two Stories by Jed Griswold
Illustrated by Jerry Aissis

Copyright © 2022 by Jed Griswold

All rights reserved. No part of this book may be reproduced in any form or by any electronic or mechanical means, including information storage and retrieval systems, without written permission from the author, except in the case of a reviewer, who may quote brief passages embodied in critical articles or in a review. The information in this book is distributed on an "as is" basis, without warranty. Although every precaution has been taken in the preparation of this work, neither the author nor the publisher shall have any liability to any person or entity with respect to any loss or damage caused or alleged to be caused directly or indirectly by the information contained in this book.

ISBN: 978-1-959957-10-2 (Hardcover)
ISBN: 978-1-959957-11-9 (Paperback)

Original stories by Jed Griswold
Format, design and editing by Jed Griswold
Original watercolor illustrations by Jerry Aissis

About the Author

Dr. Jed Griswold is a published author, a retired college administrator and Professor of Psychology, a retired minister, and currently an educational and organizational consultant living in New England. For information, contact Jed at info@griswoldconsulting.net or visit www.griswoldconsulting.net

About the Illustrator

Jerry Aissis is a retired teacher who is known for bright and bold colors in his landscapes and seascapes. He teaches art classes and displays his artwork in many New England venues. "There is inspiration all around you. Never stop looking. Never stop painting." Visit
https://FineArtAmerica.com

A Note to Parents and Teachers

A separate resource book is available for each of these two stories, written for parents and teachers. Each includes a summary from educational psychology about the central theme of the story, for *The Little Drop of Water* – facing changes in our lives, and for *Leafy the Leaf* – being ready to hold on or let go.
It also offers an educationally effective and appropriate approach to processing each story with one child or a group of children.

The Little Drop of Water - A Resource Guide for Parents and Teachers

Leafy the Leaf - A Resource Guide for Parents and Teachers

By Dr. Jed Griswold

Published by Griswold Consulting

In paperback and Kindle formats

Also by this Author

A Great Retirement, Griswold Consulting
In Between, Griswold Consulting
Leafy the Leaf, paperback, Griswold Consulting
The Little Drop of Water, paperback, Griswold Consulting
The Power of Storytelling, Wood Lake Publishing
Who Haunts This House? Griswold Consulting

The Little Drop of Water

Story by Jed Griswold
Illustrations by Jerry Aissis

Once upon a time,
there was a
little drop of water
who lived in a
very large ocean.

It loved being a part
of such a large
and diverse
community.

It would swim
with little fish --
and share
in the fun
of waves
and bubbles.

The little drop of water
would even swim
with giant whales,
and sometimes find
a peaceful rest
by diving deeper
under the big ocean.

One day,
the little drop of water
felt itself being pulled
way up into the sky,
toward a cloud.

It didn't understand how or why it was changing.

And the little drop
of water
thought
to itself,

"This is it –
my life must be over..."

But the little
drop of water
soon learned...

...that being part
of a cloud was both
fun and interesting.

The view
of the earth below
was so awesome,

the little drop
of water
smiled as much as
any drop of water
could ever smile!

But then ---

The little drop of
water-turned-cloud
changed _again_

and became
a droplet of water...
and began to fall.

At first, it thought
it was returning
to the ocean,
until it realized
that it was raining
upon a field
of vegetables.

And once again,
the little drop
of water
thought
to itself,

"This is it –
my life must be over..."

But the little drop
of water
was happy to learn
that its landing
on the ground
was not very bumpy
at all.

In fact, the garden
of vegetables
was as soft as a bed.

But the little drop of water was still confused.

"Why did I land on the ground instead of back in the ocean?"

But after visiting
with the vegetables,
and some humans
who gathered them,
the little drop of water
quickly learned how much
they needed water,
to grow strong and
tasty.

As the sun smiled, the little drop of water had an idea that there were more changes to come.

But this time,
the little drop of water
had a bigger view of life
in the bigger world
we all live in ...
and it was already
wondering ...

"what will change next?"

What Are You Thinking About?

what is your favorite part of this story? why?

what do you think was the drop of water's hardest change?

what did the drop of water learn from this experience?

what changed in the story, from beginning to end?

What Are You Feeling?

Have you ever experienced changes, like the little drop of water did?

Who helps you when changes happen to you?

How do you help others who experience changes?

What will you remember about this story?

What Do You Wonder About?

Do you wonder what changes the drop of water might experience in the future?

Do you wonder about how the drop of water felt during its changes?

Even though the drop of water changed, do you wonder about what stayed the same?

Do you wonder about what the drop of water would share with you about this experience?

Leafy the Leaf

Story by Jed Griswold
Illustrations by Jerry Aissis

Once upon a time
there lived
a happy leaf
named Leafy.

Leafy was a regular leaf who liked regular leaf activities —

Such as...

Swinging in the breeze,

waving to the birds
and butterflies, and

feeling the sun's rays.

And Leafy especially
enjoyed listening
to the interesting
gathering of humans
who stopped by
to rest at
Leafy's tree trunk.

But there was
a problem.

When the weather started to change, and the days started to grow shorter, Leafy wasn't ready.

The wind
started saying,
"It's fall, Leafy ...
so fall, Leafy,"
but Leafy
wasn't ready.

And when
the wind's voice
got louder,
and other leaves
started to let go...

Leafy's ears
closed tightly ...
and Leafy held on
just as tightly.

"I won't let go.
I'll never let go."

Even when
Leafy was
the only one left
on a big branch,
feeling all alone,

Leafy still held on.

As the wind got
bolder and bolder,
Leafy got
stiffer and stiffer.

But Leafy still held on.

The weather got
colder and colder,
and Leafy got _more_
stiffer and stiffer.

But Leafy _still_ held on.

A wise piece of cover
on the tree,
named Bark,
voiced some wisdom
in saying out loud,

"Sometimes it is good
to hold on,
and sometimes it is
the right time
to let go."

So Bark barked out,

"It's fall, Leafy,
it's the right time
to let go.

So let go
and fall, Leafy!"

But Leafy's
eyes closed
and Leafy
held on
as tightly
as tight
could ever be.

And then happened.

None of the birds,
or even the few
butterflies who had
stayed around
to support Leafy –

None of them knew
why ...

But Leafy
was now ready
to let go.

And to Leafy's
surprise,
the fall
toward the base
of the tree
was a very pleasant
adventure.

No longer
stiff and tight,
Leafy flew gently
like a bird, and
slowly like a butterfly,

to join a wonderful
party of Leafy's
friends, playing
in a pile of leaves
at the base
of the tree.

What Are You Thinking About?

What is your favorite part of this story? Why?

Why do you think Leafy kept holding on?

What do you think Leafy learned from this experience?

What changed in the story, from beginning to end?

What Are You Feeling?

Have you ever experienced something like Leafy did?

Who helped you when you experienced something like Leafy did?

How do you help others who experience something like Leafy did?

What will you remember about this story?

What Do You Wonder About?

Do you wonder what other times
Leafy might face the same experience
in the future?

Do you wonder about how Leafy felt
during this experience?

Even though Leafy let go of something,
do you wonder about what Leafy held on to?

Do you wonder about what Leafy would
share with you about this experience?

Made in the USA
Middletown, DE
18 January 2023

22356704R00046